How to Sell eBa

The Essential Handbook for New Sellers: From Listing to Shipping: Everything You Need to Know to Start Selling, including over 20 products to list and start making sales instantly.

By

Elmer Brian Ralph

Copyright © 2024

Table of Contents

Introduction 5

1 10

    How to set up your eBay account and profile 10

2 17

    How to find and source products to sell on eBay 17

        Dropshipping 17

        Hard Truths About Dropshipping 19

        The Effective Strategies for Dropshipping 24

        Wholesale 31

        White label and private label 37

        Popular Private-Label Manufacturers 65

3 76

    How to create compelling and optimized listings that converts. 76

        Titles 76

        Descriptions 77

        How to Take and Edit High-Quality Photos for eBay 80

        How to Choose the Right Category, Condition, and Price Selling on eBay 83

        How to price your products for maximum profit and sales 86

4 97

    How to manage your inventory and shipping 97

        Organizing and storing your products 97

        Packing and shipping your products 98

        Tracking and updating your orders 99

        Handling returns and refunds 100

5 102

How to provide excellent customer service and build your reputation 102

Communication is key 102

Responding to questions, feedback, and complaints 104

Resolving disputes and cases 105

Earning positive ratings and reviews 107

6 110

How to grow your EBay business and scale up your income 110

Cross-Sell and Upsell Your Products 110

Product Bundling 111

Discounts and promotions 111

Product range expansion 112

Diversify your income streams 113

Leveraging other platforms and tools 114

Social media and e-commerce 116

Organic and paid social 117

Social media marketing tips 118

Marketing with videos 120

Conclusion 125

Introduction

Welcome to my book, "How to Sell on eBay. In this book, you will learn everything you need to know to start and grow your own successful online business using the world's largest marketplace, eBay.

Selling on eBay is a great opportunity for anyone who wants to make money online. Whether you are looking for a side hustle, a full-time income, or a way to turn your passion into profit, eBay has something for you. You can sell almost anything on eBay, from new and used items, to collectibles and antiques, to digital products and services. You can reach millions of buyers around the world, and enjoy the flexibility and freedom of being your own boss.

But selling on eBay is not as easy as it sounds. There are many challenges and pitfalls that you need to avoid, such as finding the right products to sell, pricing them competitively, creating attractive listings, handling shipping and returns, dealing with customer service issues, and complying with eBay's policies and regulations. You also need to know how to market your products effectively, how to optimize your store for search engines, how to use social media and email marketing to build your brand and loyal customer base, and how to scale your business to the next level.

This and many other reasons compelled me to write this book. I have been selling on eBay for over 10 years, and I have learned a lot from my own successes and failures. In this book, I will share with you all my tips, tricks, strategies, and best practices that I have discovered and tested over the years. I will teach you how to sell on eBay like a pro, and how to avoid the common mistakes that most beginners make.

This book is suitable for anyone who wants to sell on eBay, regardless of your experience level, budget, or niche. Whether you are a complete beginner who has never sold anything online before, or an experienced seller who wants to improve your skills and results, this book will help you achieve your goals. This book is also up-to-date with the latest trends, technologies, and changes that affect the eBay marketplace.

In this book, you will learn:

- How to set up your eBay account and store

- How to find profitable products to sell on eBay

- How to source products from wholesalers, dropshippers, liquidators, or your own inventory

- How to price your products for maximum profit and sales

- How to create compelling listings that attract buyers and convert them into customers

- How to take professional photos and videos of your products

- How to write captivating titles and descriptions that rank well on eBay's search engine

- How to use keywords and tags to optimize your listings for SEO

- How to offer free shipping and returns without losing money

- How to handle payments, taxes, invoices, and receipts

- How to ship your products quickly and safely

- How to deal with refunds, disputes, feedback, and reviews

- How to provide excellent customer service and build trust and loyalty

- How to use eBay's tools and features to manage your store efficiently

- How to use analytics and reports to track your performance and improve your strategy

- How to market your products using social media, email marketing, blogs, podcasts, YouTube videos, and more

- How to grow your audience and customer base using contests, giveaways, coupons, discounts, referrals, testimonials, and more

- How to scale your business using automation tools, outsourcing services, virtual assistants, or employees

- How to diversify your income streams using other platforms such as Amazon FBA (Fulfillment by Amazon), Shopify (an ecommerce platform), Etsy (a marketplace for handmade goods), or Udemy (an online learning platform)

- And much more!

By the end of this book, you will have all the knowledge and skills you need to start selling on eBay with confidence and success. You will also have a clear action plan that you can follow step by step to launch your online business in no time.

So, what are you waiting for? Grab your copy of this book today and get ready to sell on eBay like a pro!

1
How to set up your eBay account and profile

Welcome to the first chapter of our guide on how to sell on eBay. In this chapter, we will show you how to set up your eBay account and profile, which are essential steps to start your online selling journey. Here are the topics we will cover in this chapter:

- Creating an account

- Choosing a username

- Verifying your identity

- Setting up your payment methods

- Optimizing your profile for buyers

Creating an account

Creating an account

To create an account on eBay, you need to have a valid email address and a phone number. You can sign up using your Facebook, Google, or Apple account, or you can create a new account with your email address. To sign up with your email address, follow these steps:

- Go to the eBay homepage and click on the Register link at the top left corner of the page.

- Enter your first and last name, your email address, and a password of your choice. Make sure your password is strong and secure, and that you can remember it easily.

- Click on the Create account button.

You will receive a confirmation email from eBay with a link to verify your email address. Click on the link to complete the verification process. You will also receive a text message from eBay with a code to verify your phone number. Enter the code on the eBay website to complete the verification process.

Choosing a username

Your username is how you will be identified on eBay. It is also part of your profile URL, which you can share with potential buyers to showcase your listings and feedback. Therefore, it is important for you to choose a username and it should be unique, memorable, and appropriate for the marketplace. To choose a username, follow these steps:

- Go to My eBay and click on Account settings.

- Click on Personal information on the left side of the page.

- Under User ID, click on Edit.

- Enter a new username of your choice. You can use letters, numbers, underscores, and hyphens, but no spaces or special characters. Your username must be between 6 and 64 characters long.

- Click on Save.

You can change your username once every 30 days. However, we recommend that you choose a username that you are happy with and stick with it, as changing it too often may confuse or deter your buyers.

Verifying your identity

To sell on eBay, you need to verify your identity with a government-issued ID, such as a driver's license or a passport. This helps us ensure that our marketplace is safe and secure for both buyers and sellers. To verify your identity, follow these steps:

- Go to My eBay and click on Account settings.

- Click on Personal information on the left side of the page.

- Under Identity confirmation, click on Verify.

- Choose the type of ID you want to use and follow the instructions to upload a photo or scan of it.

- Click on Submit.

You will receive a confirmation email from eBay once your ID has been verified. This may take up to 48 hours. You can check the status of your verification on the same page where you submitted your ID.

Setting up your payment methods

The goal of selling on eBay is to make money and thus to receive payments from your buyers, you need to set up your payment methods on eBay platform. The default and preferred payment method on the eBay platform is PayPal, which is a secure and convenient way to send and receive money online. To set up PayPal as your payment method, follow these steps:

- Go to My eBay and click on Account settings.

- Click on PayPal Account on the left side of the page.

- Click on Link My PayPal Account.

- Sign in to your PayPal account or create a new one if you don't have one already.

- Click on Agree and Link.

When you are done linking your Paypal, you will be redirected back to eBay and see a confirmation message that your PayPal account has been linked. You can now receive payments from buyers directly to your PayPal account.

You can also add other payment methods, such as credit cards, debit cards, or bank transfers, depending on your country and currency. If you need to add other payment methods, follow these steps:

- Go to My eBay and click on Account settings.

- Click on Payment options on the left side of the page.

- Click on Add payment method.

- Choose the payment method you want to add and follow the instructions to enter the required information.

- Click on Save.

You can add up to 8 payment methods to your account. You can also choose which payment methods you want to accept for each listing when you create or edit it.

Optimizing your profile for buyers

As a seller, you shouldn't neglect your profile, a professionally set up profile can speak volume and entice customers. The many reasons why you would want to set up your profile is because your profile is where you can showcase yourself as a seller and build trust with your buyers. Your profile includes information such as:

- Your username

- Your profile picture

- Your location

- Your feedback score and rating

- Your bio

- Your listings

- Your collections

- Your followers

To optimize your profile for buyers, follow these tips:

- Choose a username that reflects what you sell or who you are as a seller.

- Upload a clear and professional profile picture that represents you or your brand.

- Fill out your location with your city and country, so buyers can see where you are shipping from.

- Maintain a high feedback score and rating by providing excellent customer service and delivering on your promises.

- Write a bio that introduces yourself and your business, and highlights your unique selling proposition or value proposition.

- Create and update your listings with clear and accurate titles, descriptions, photos, prices, shipping options, and return policies.

- Create and curate collections of items that you sell or like, and give them catchy names and descriptions.

- Follow other sellers and buyers who share your interests or niche, and interact with them by liking, commenting, or sharing their items or collections.

By following these steps, you will have a complete and attractive profile that will help you attract more buyers and increase your sales on eBay.

2

How to find and source products to sell on eBay

Although, there are many ecommerce platforms to sell your products but if you want to start an online business, selling products on eBay is a great option. With eBay, you the ability of reaching millions of buyers, setting your own prices, and most importantly, working from anywhere. But before you can start selling there, you need to find and source products that are in demand, profitable, and easy to ship. You don't just put in anything on eBay and expect it to sell. In this chapter, we will discuss the different ways of finding products, such as dropshipping, wholesale, retail arbitrage, thrift stores, garage sales, etc. We will also explain how to evaluate the demand, competition, and profitability of each product niche.

Dropshipping

We're all familiar with Dropshipping, but if you're not, this guide is here to help you out. It's tailored for those who are contemplating launching an eBay dropshipping business but lack the essential knowledge or know-how to get started. Within the pages of this book, you'll uncover invaluable tips, strategies, and insights gleaned from experienced sellers who've successfully journeyed from zero to $5,000 in profit within just eight months with their eBay dropshipping ventures.

Before diving into your dropshipping venture, it's crucial to:

- Allocate a modest budget for your initial setup and any required software subscriptions.
- Get acquainted with eBay's dropshipping policies to ensure compliance.

Understanding eBay Dropshipping:

Dropshipping is a method of fulfilling orders where you don't need to maintain inventory. In this approach, you market the product and relay the sales order to a third-party supplier, who then handles shipping directly to the customer.

While many believe it's the fastest route to profit in business, dropshipping isn't a shortcut to wealth. It entails more than simply selling others' products and taking a share of the profits; you also need to contend with various challenges, setbacks, and daily operational tasks. Recognizing these factors reveals that dropshipping isn't straightforward and often demands considerable effort.

Nonetheless, when executed properly, dropshipping can still facilitate the establishment of a successful business—albeit not as swiftly as initially anticipated.

Hard Truths About Dropshipping

For business owners looking to streamline their online store's product shipping process, particularly those running traditional retail operations such as t-shirt sales, the dropshipping model presents a viable solution. Crucially, it can enhance the efficiency of an ecommerce store.

Once a customer completes an online purchase, the dropshipping business handles the direct shipment of the product to the customer. This method allows both large and small companies to procure products while generating income and saving storage space concurrently.

Nevertheless, this approach comes with its own set of challenges. Thus, it's vital to grasp the reasons behind its demanding nature before committing all your savings to a dropshipping venture.

1. Low profit margins.

You're probably aware that with dropshipping, you won't need to handle or store your own inventory, resulting in low overhead costs and reduced returns. However, it operates on a "garbage in, garbage out" principle, meaning that investing less money often yields less profit. Ironically, despite needing a high volume of sales to stay afloat, let alone make a profit, a significant portion of revenue typically goes to the supplier.

Over time, you'll find that these slim profit margins are insufficient to cover expenses like marketing, website maintenance (including SEO), order management, and office hours.

You can estimate your income using these variables (though they're averages and may vary based on your industry and circumstances):

With a 20% margin and a 2% conversion rate, you can estimate your profit using the equation: (Traffic x 0.02) x (Avg order value x 0.2) = Profit.

However, this serves as a starting estimate and overlooks several important considerations:

- Your discounts from manufacturers and wholesalers may be less than 20%.
- Additional expenses mentioned earlier, such as marketing and operational costs, are not factored into this calculation.
- Some products may require reducing your profit margins to stay competitive, risking being undercut by competitors.
- Profit is heavily influenced by traffic, especially when building an ecommerce brand from scratch on platforms like BigCommerce and Shopify, where acquiring a client base can be challenging.
- Despite the perception of dropshipping being hands-off, it involves ongoing management of wholesale suppliers, order processing, returns, and customer service.
- It's more feasible to pursue dropshipping when you already have a steady stream of traffic.

2. Highly competitive.

There will always be overly optimistic entrepreneurs who focus on the "low overhead" aspect while overlooking the evident challenges. With the minimal capital required to start a dropshipping venture, the entry barrier is low, leading to fierce competition, especially in popular markets.

In essence, larger companies have the capability to drastically reduce their markups, offering the most competitive prices. Moreover, securing an exclusive agreement with your suppliers is unlikely. Consequently, numerous competitors might be selling identical products. As a small business just starting out, your more established rivals have the resources to undercut your prices.

This scenario sets the stage for potential customers to find the same products elsewhere at a lower cost, raising the question: why would they opt to purchase from you?

3. Limited control over the supply chain.

In a traditional ecommerce setup where you manage operations, you can swiftly respond to customer concerns regarding product quality, shipping speed, or return policies. However, in the dropshipping model, store owners heavily rely on suppliers—yet remain responsible for customer interactions.

As a dropshipper, you're essentially restricted, relying on suppliers to resolve issues while simultaneously reassuring customers about aspects beyond your influence. Additionally, communication with suppliers may be less efficient, resulting in delays in resolving problems if responses are slow.

Furthermore, if customers express dissatisfaction, especially on social media platforms, negative reviews early on could jeopardize the success of your business before it gains momentum.

4. Legal risks

Though not commonly encountered by dropshippers, it's crucial to acknowledge. Certain suppliers may not uphold the level of credibility they claim, and the sourcing of merchandise may lack transparency.

Of greater concern is the unauthorized use of trademarked logos or intellectual property belonging to other companies, a scenario that arises more frequently than anticipated.

To mitigate this risk, implementing a comprehensive Dropshipping Agreement Contract is essential. However, not all newcomers to dropshipping are familiar with this precautionary measure. It's a factor to be mindful of when choosing suppliers.

5. Brand building hurdles

Like ghostwriters or undisclosed songwriters, dropshippers need to recognize that their efforts are often attributed to others.

When you sell exceptional products, customers typically attribute them to the product's brand, often disregarding the shopping experience entirely. Since your logo isn't on the packaging, this poses a challenge.

This emphasizes why dropshipping is typically better suited for established brands rather than new ones.

The Effective Strategies for Dropshipping

Dropshipping is most effective when viewed as a supplementary aspect rather than the primary focal point of a business. Although its limitations pose challenges for sustaining a business solely on this model, it still presents ample advantages to significantly bolster ecommerce ventures.

To optimize the utilization of this business model, the following four strategies should be considered:

1. Conducting thorough market research.

Dropshipping proves more beneficial when utilized as a means to an end rather than an end goal in itself. Employ dropshipping to mitigate the risks associated with testing new products and conducting market research.

Instead of incurring high inventory costs by stocking uncertain products in your warehouse, experiment with them through dropshipping. This approach not only aids in determining their sales potential but also offers a more precise estimate of their selling price, facilitating the determination of initial stock quantity.

This becomes particularly vital when delving into new product categories, which inherently carry risks. For instance, if you've found success in selling dog products, would the same apply to cat products?

Although uncertainties exist, interest levels can be gauged by dropshipping a selection of products and assessing their performance.

2. Preventing Overstocking

Seasoned ecommerce brands understand that market fluctuations can be unpredictable. Rather than inflating inventory costs by stockpiling to meet unlikely maximums, having a dropshipping supplier as a backup can save you money without sacrificing potential sales.

This is particularly beneficial for managing seasonal overflow and serves as a valuable safeguard against the uncertainties all retailers encounter.

Having dropshipping alternatives in place also provides excellent insurance against extraordinary circumstances. In the event of a natural disaster affecting your warehouse space, for instance, you can still fulfill pre-existing orders by dropshipping products from alternative locations. Similarly, it serves as a contingency plan for navigating unexpected shipping delays.

3. Strategic Shipping Solutions

Expanding your business often leads to shipping complexities. As your reach extends further from your warehouse or fulfillment centers, shipping costs and fees tend to increase.

Dropshipping can offer an ideal solution for addressing shipping challenges in problematic locations outside your core profitable regions. Whether it's due to high shipping costs, prohibitive storage expenses for setting up new shipping centers, or issues like taxes and additional fees associated with shipping across state or international borders, relying on dropshipping for these specific areas could be crucial in maintaining profitability.

Furthermore, just as dropshipping proves useful in market research, it can also serve as a tool for testing new markets. Why not utilize dropshipping for a trial period in a new location to assess its viability before committing to establishing a new facility there?

4. Handling High-Maintenance Products

Certain products entail higher costs related to inventory management and shipping.

In certain situations, opting for dropshipping may yield greater profitability compared to maintaining inventory in-house.

What characterizes high-maintenance products?

These encompass items that result in added expenses for storage or shipping, including:

- Bulky products: Some items require substantial space, rendering their sales insufficient to offset storage costs.

- Weighty products: If shipping expenses are disproportionately high due to weight, sourcing through dropshipping directly from manufacturers or wholesalers could be advantageous.

- Fragile products: Items prone to damage during transit necessitate specialized handling, often best managed by suppliers or manufacturers.

- Valuable items: High-value goods like fine jewelry or antiques demand heightened security measures not universally available in all storage facilities. Delegating storage to a capable entity reduces the risk of theft.

- Products with specific requirements: Items needing particular storage conditions, such as frozen goods or light-sensitive materials, may be more effectively managed via dropshipping rather than in-house storage.

Unless your business exclusively focuses on these product categories, bearing additional storage and shipping expenses for a small portion of your operations is impractical.

However, you can still fulfill customer demands by offering these products through dropshipping.

Choosing the Optimal Dropshipping Suppliers

When integrating dropshipping into your sales strategy, you're essentially forming a business partnership with the supplier, regardless of the scale. As previously mentioned, as the vendor, you heavily rely on your dropshipper for product quality, timely shipping, and adherence to legal standards. Therefore, it's imperative to select your suppliers with utmost care.

Your primary goal is to ensure that the products match their advertised specifications, while also assessing if their shipping methods meet your requirements. Apart from product quality, there are various other factors to consider regarding your supplier's business practices.

Below is a convenient checklist of inquiries to consider before establishing a partnership with a supplier:

- How do they handle returns or manage damaged products?

- What is their order fulfillment timeframe, from purchase to delivery?

- How efficient is their customer support? (Consider conducting your own test.)

- Do they offer insurance for orders?

- Is fraud protection available?

- Are there any reviews or references accessible online?

Furthermore, remember to thoroughly review the Dropshipping Agreement Contract, as previously discussed.

To streamline your research process, we've previously compiled a list of reputable dropshipping companies, including Spocket and AliExpress Dropshipping.

Do I need to register a business entity for dropshipping?

Yes, you'll need to register your business once your sales reach a certain level. However, there's no immediate need until your sales become consistent. This is because most payment providers typically require proof of such credentials for your business."

The advantages of dropshipping are:

- You can sell a wide variety of products without having to invest in them.

- You can test different products and niches without risking money.

- You can scale your business quickly and easily.

The disadvantages of dropshipping are:

- You have less control over the product quality, availability, and delivery time.

- You have to deal with customer service issues such as refunds, returns, and complaints.

- You have to compete with other dropshippers who may sell the same products at lower prices.

To succeed with dropshipping, you need to find a reliable supplier who can offer you high-quality products at competitive prices. You also need to do market research to find profitable niches and keywords that attract buyers. You can use tools like Google Trends, eBay's Advanced Search, and Terapeak to analyze the demand, competition, and profitability of different products and niches.

Wholesale

Wholesale is a method of buying products in bulk from a manufacturer or distributor at a discounted price. You then resell the products on eBay at a higher price. Unlike dropshipping, you have to buy and store the products yourself before you can sell them. This means you have to invest more money upfront and deal with inventory management.

For instance, suppose you intend to retail name-brand toy cars typically priced at $15 each. If you opt not to go through a wholesaler, you might negotiate a purchasing price of $12 per car directly from the manufacturer, provided you buy 75 cars monthly. This would yield a profit of $3 per car.

However, if you procure the same products from a wholesaler who acquired 40,000 cars at a substantially lower price of $5 per car, they could sell 75 cars to you at $10 each, generating a profit of $5 per car for them. Consequently, when you sell the cars on eBay at $15 each, you still retain the same profit margin.

There's no guarantee that the products acquired from a wholesaler will achieve successful sales. However, when making your purchase, ensure that the items obtained from your wholesaler uphold a high standard of quality. While it's feasible to find wholesale products from liquidation or estate sales, their quality may not consistently meet top-tier standards.

Many people commonly view eBay as a platform mainly for acquiring collectibles, gently used items, and vintage designer goods. However, what they might overlook is that 80 percent of the items available on eBay are actually brand new. Interestingly, numerous eBay sellers invest considerable time in sourcing products for sale on alternative platforms. Surprisingly, one of the most effective places to discover items for sale on eBay is eBay itself, whether through purchasing inventory or selling bulk lots of merchandise.

Sources of Wholesale and Bulk Lots

Wholesale lots originate from a variety of channels, such as liquidators, manufacturers, retail stores, estate auctions, and fellow eBay sellers. It's important to exercise caution when purchasing lots labeled with terms like "liquidator" or "liquidation," as these items could potentially be damaged or of lower quality. Occasionally, items are liquidated from businesses due to legal mandates or closures. If the liquidator is compelled to swiftly sell off assets to settle debts, the items may not be in optimal condition or could be damaged. Therefore, always carefully scrutinize the product description, inspect the photos thoroughly, and review the return policy. You wouldn't want to end up with excess inventory that proves challenging to sell.

Keep an Eye on the Content of Bulk Lots

Some wholesale lots are listed by manufacturers or suppliers, while others are collections of items put together by eBay sellers. For example, a seller, probably a mother who have had grown up children might gather 50 pieces shoes with different styles, sizes, and brands of those her children when they were kids and put them up for sale on eBay.

Unfortunately, eBay doesn't check the keywords of wholesale lots to make sure they're genuine wholesale items. Many sellers may not realize that using the term "wholesale" could be misleading. In such cases, it's better to call them "shoes lot" or "bulk lot."

When searching for inventory lots to resell, it's important to watch out for the misuse of the term "wholesale" on eBay. Make sure to message the seller on eBay to ask about where the items in the lot came from or to confirm if they're really wholesale.

Categories for Wholesale Lots

In the past, eBay had one category for all wholesale lots. However, now wholesale lot categories are subcategories under clothing, jewelry, crafts, supplies, etc. For example, to find wholesale jewelry lots, go to the Jewelry and Watches category and choose the wholesale lots subcategory. There are over 75,000 items for sale, ranging from $1 auctions to $50,000 Harry Winston diamond watches.

Another category with lots of wholesale items is Crafts, which has over 50,000 listings for bulk craft supplies. Similarly, the Clothing, Shoes, and Accessories category has over 50,000 items in the wholesale lot subcategory. The Health and Beauty category also offers over 10,000 items in the wholesale lot subcategory.

Consider Buying Lots for Disassembling

If you are a seller and you are having trouble finding inventory, buying lots on eBay is a great way to get inventory. Many eBay sellers start selling because they're sick, disabled, or taking care of someone, which makes it hard for them to work outside the home.

For people with physical limitations or living in rural areas with limited inventory access, buying lots on eBay creates opportunities for making money. Known as "virtual picking," buying easy-to-find items on eBay for resale is a good strategy. Bulk lots of inventory, drawer lots, and leftover estate sale items can be bought, taken apart, and the individual pieces or parts resold for profit. Estate sale buy-out companies often don't have time to sell each item separately, while other sellers who are homebound have time and motivation to go through lots and take them apart.

The advantages of wholesale are:

- You have more control over the product quality, availability, and delivery time.

- You can build your own brand and reputation by selling unique or exclusive products.

- You can negotiate better prices and terms with your suppliers.

The disadvantages of wholesale are:

- You have to invest more money upfront and risk losing it if the products don't sell.

- You have to deal with inventory management issues such as storage space, packaging, and shipping.

- You have to compete with other wholesalers who may sell the same products at lower prices.

To succeed with wholesale, you need to find a trustworthy supplier who can offer you high-quality products at low prices. You also need to do market research to find profitable niches and keywords that attract buyers. You can use tools like Google Trends, eBay's Advanced Search, and Terapeak to analyze the demand, competition, and profitability of different products and niches.

White label and private label

In the business and marketing landscape, white label and private label concepts are often viewed as methods for expanding brands and distinguishing products. Although they may appear similar initially, each approach provides unique benefits and addresses specific business requirements. Grasping the differences between white label and private label is vital for companies seeking to employ these strategies to enhance growth and maintain a competitive edge.

White Label

White labeling means a company creates a product or service and sells it to another company. The buyer, called the white label brand owner, then sells the product under their own brand. Essentially, white labeling is about taking an existing product from one company and putting your own brand on it.

The term 'white labeling' stems from the notion of a blank label on a product's packaging, which can be filled in with the marketer's brand details. It's a mutually beneficial arrangement: manufacturers can produce goods at scale without concerning themselves with the marketing aspect, and marketers can offer products without the overhead of manufacturing.

While this might seem simple, understanding why white labeling is important in today's business world requires a closer look.

One of the key advantages of white labeling is the ability to quickly enter the market with new products under an established brand name, which can foster customer trust and loyalty. It also enables companies to diversify their product offerings and target specific market segments without the risk and expense associated with developing new products from scratch.

Retail giants like Walmart and Whole Foods have successfully leveraged white labeling to offer exclusive store brands that appeal to price-sensitive consumers while maintaining a perception of quality. These store brands often compete with national brands on the shelves, providing consumers with more choices and often at lower prices.

In today's business world, the concept of white labeling has become more practical. This applies to businesses of all sizes, as the market for white-labeled products continues to grow. Developers now offer increasingly specialized solutions, with prices ranging from a few hundred to several thousand dollars per month. Essentially, white labeling in business refers to a ready-to-market solution that is fully developed, highly competitive, and offered on a regular rental model, complete with comprehensive technical support and expert guidance.

Launching a white-labeled product requires significant effort and time, even for those who have progressed beyond the planning stage. Building brand recognition and cultivating a loyal customer base further extend the timeline. Therefore, the emergence of the white label business model addresses this challenge. Instead of spending years developing a competitive product from scratch, businesses can adapt existing technology and rebrand it within a matter of weeks.

However, diving into the complexities of white labeling reveals that it's not as simple as it may appear. In this article, we will explore these nuances in detail.

White Label Branding

White label branding means creating products and services and then rebranding and marketing them under another brand's name. The main goal is to build customer loyalty and trust while saving time and resources needed for developing new solutions.

For business growth, white labeling is helpful for startups and businesses that haven't established their own competitive brand identities but already offer products or services of comparable or better quality. For other companies, using a white label approach allows them to focus on product development without spending resources on marketing. Essentially, a "white label business" refers to a product or service created by one company but sold by another.

A white label product is basically a generic item that gets rebranded and customized with the purchasing company's logo, label, and identity to be used as their own. This reduces upfront capital investment for the buyer, as the vendor takes care of things like software licensing, server space, logistics, and technical support. Once the product is customized with the buyer's brand identity, they can start selling it under their own name, making money and sharing profits with the service provider.

So, how does the white labeling process work exactly? The vendor company creates a ready-to-use product tailored to the buyer's business needs, like a white-label advertising platform that matches the buyer's brand seamlessly. The buyer then adds their company's name, logo, icons, URLs, emails, text, and website elements to customize the product to their brand. Once everything is customized, the buyer can start selling the white-label product under their own terms and conditions.

Reasons Your Business Should Try White Labeling

1. Saves Money: Building something from scratch can be costly. With white label software, you can launch your own branded platforms with all the latest features without spending too much on custom development.

2. Get Tech Help: White label platforms come with full technical support from the provider. This means you don't have to worry about managing the technical stuff yourself – they've got you covered.

3. Focus on Marketing: White labeling frees up your resources so you can concentrate on promoting your brand and improving customer service while the provider handles the technical side of things.

4. Easy Tech Management: White label solutions handle all the technical complexities, so you don't need a big team to customize or update them, especially if you're in the software business.

5. No Licensing Hassles: White label products help you skip the hassle of dealing with special licenses, so you can put more effort into selling and promoting your products.

6. Customize Without Building: You can create unique solutions that match your goals and customer service needs without starting from scratch.

7. Grow Your Business: White label solutions can grow and change with your business, letting you tweak features and improve functionality as you go.

8. Own Your Solution: Partnering with white label providers means you get to own and control your custom platforms, giving you long-term control and value.

In short, white label solutions offer lots of benefits like saving money, getting tech support, customizing easily, and growing with your business, making them a smart choice for improving your business and getting noticed in the market.

Examples of White Label Products

White label branding can be seen in various industries, from fashion to technology, where manufacturers produce goods in bulk, then rebranded and sold by different retailers.

Coffee:

The coffee industry is a great example of white labeling. Large-scale producers roast beans in factories and distribute them to retailers. These retailers, which include online stores and local coffee shops, present the coffee as their own, even though they all come from the same white label manufacturer.

Skin Care:

In skincare, white label brands are common. Moisturizers, serums, and other products are made by one manufacturer, then packaged and labeled differently by different skincare companies. Some may add unique ingredients, but the basic formula remains the same.

Software:

White label software is widely used in the technology sector, especially in SaaS (software as a service). Companies put their branding on software developed by others, often adding extra features or services before selling it as their own.

Telecommunications Companies and Retailers

These companies can expand their product offerings by introducing branded smartphones to their customers without having to develop them from scratch. This allows them to compete more effectively in the market and cater to specific customer preferences. Additionally, they can strengthen brand loyalty by offering exclusive devices under their own branding.

The Impact of White Labeling on Consumer Choice

One of the primary impacts of white labeling on consumer choice is the expansion of available options. When retailers can brand and sell products as their own, they can quickly diversify their offerings to meet consumer demands. This means more choices for consumers, both in terms of product variety and price points. For instance, a consumer may find a white-labeled product that offers similar quality to a well-known brand but at a more affordable price, which can be particularly appealing to budget-conscious shoppers.

However, white labeling can also lead to confusion among consumers. With multiple retailers selling similar or identical products under different brand names, it can be challenging for consumers to make informed decisions. This is especially true when there is a lack of transparency about the origins of white-labeled products. Consumers may not be aware that the same manufacturer produces multiple brands, which can lead to a false perception of variety and competition in the market.

Moreover, white labeling can influence consumer trust. Brands often build their reputation over time through consistent quality and customer service. When a product is white-labeled, consumers may place their trust in the retailer's brand without knowing much about the actual manufacturer. If the product fails to meet expectations, it can affect the consumer's trust in the retailer, even though the retailer may not be directly responsible for the product's manufacturing.

In terms of consumer behavior, studies have shown that labeling can significantly impact purchasing decisions. While these studies focus on specific types of labeling, they highlight the broader point that how products are presented to consumers—including through white labeling—can shape their purchasing decisions.

Tips for Selling White Labels on eBay

eBay is like the go-to spot for buying and selling those white-label products because it's got a ton of options at good prices and a bunch of loyal customers. Some sellers might be nervous about all the price battles that come with selling basic stuff, but this book will show you how to make good money and keep those sales coming in.

DETERMINE HOW POPULAR WHITE LABEL PRODUCTS ARE IN THE CATEGORY

Although white label products are currently trending, not all categories will experience the same level of success. This highlights consumers' willingness to invest in such items. However, certain categories, such as baby hats, dog supplies, and women's shoes, are especially popular for white-label goods, constituting over 30% of total sales. It's crucial to assess the demand for white-label products within your specific niche before committing to selling them.

UNDERSTAND THE PRICE POINTS THAT BUYERS ARE PURCHASING AT

On eBay, there's a widespread belief that white-label products face tough price competition, which makes some sellers hesitant to venture into selling them due to worries about price cuts. However, this viewpoint isn't entirely accurate.

While pricing does play a role in sales, white-label products priced higher can still do well. Take, for instance, the Baby Hats and Caps category, where top white-label listings range from $1.99 to $18.49—a wide price spectrum.

Did the $1.99 product dominate sales? Not necessarily. Through experience with certain software, it's been observed that weekly sales vary across different price ranges. Data shows that most sales occur within the $3 - $4 range, closely followed by the $5 - $6 range.

IDENTIFYING PRICE POINTS WITH LESS COMPETITION

Many sellers think they should match competitors' lower prices, leading to a race to the bottom. But this isn't always the case. Instead, it's important to set prices that align with what buyers are willing to pay. In many instances, the most common price range among listings corresponds with the highest sales—the $3 - $4 range."

FIND OUT THE PRODUCT FEATURES THAT MATTER TO BUYERS

The range of features available in white-label products, even within the same category, can be vast. It's essential to select products with features that resonate with buyers.

For instance, some might assume that sales in the Baby Hats & Caps category are limited to basic options like pink, blue, and white cotton caps. However, through proper research tools, we uncover that the top-selling listing in the $4 - $5 price range is a soft cotton beanie with a large bow, priced at $4.99. Meanwhile, in the $6 - $7 price range, it's a thicker-knit beanie with oversized faux fur pom-poms, priced at $6.99. Despite both being baby beanies, they cater to different preferences, underscoring the significance of comprehending buyer needs and preferences.

STAY ON TOP OF YOUR GAME

Getting a top-notch product is just the first step. Stay alert to market shifts and utilize eBay's tools to amp up your sales. Take advantage of Promoted Listings to increase visibility, entice buyers with deals via Promotions Manager, and ensure your item details are comprehensive to help eBay grasp your product better.

Even though white-label items face tough competition on eBay, sellers can still discover profitable niches through thorough research. This entails grasping:

- How popular white label items are in your chosen categories

- Price ranges that draw in buyers

- Competition levels across different price brackets

- Product features that push sales at higher prices

- The competitive scene, which involves keeping tabs on trends, challenges, and opportunities.

Car and Truck Struts Seller Insights on eBay Motors

eBay Motors has become a thriving hub for car parts sellers, offering substantial opportunities in the car struts sector. This book provides in-depth insights derived from eBay data, aiming to assist sellers in this category in refining their strategies and achieving improved sales outcomes.

TOP SELLING PRODUCTS: WHAT'S HOT IN THE MARKET?

Our analysis of the top products highlights specific trends in terms of weekly sales, predominantly influenced by pricing factors:

1. Shock Adjustment Tools: Products like the "Fit For Rancho RS9000XL Shock Adjustment Tool" lead the pack with an average of 5.10 sales per week.

2. Vehicle-Specific Kits: Items such as "2.5" Front Ford Lift Kit Leveling Kit for 2004..." and "SR Billet 1" Front Leveling Lift Kit 04-22 For..." exhibit clear demand for solutions tailored to specific vehicles, with 3.32 and 2.59 weekly sales respectively.

This category demonstrates a trend of lower-priced items selling at a higher frequency compared to slower-selling, higher-priced products. Your choice of products to sell will depend on factors such as your capacity and the selection available from suppliers.

RETURN AND WARRANTY POLICIES: BUILDING CUSTOMER TRUST

The majority of listings allow returns, and many sellers foot the bill for return shipping. Typically, there's a 30-day return window.

Providing competitive return policies, especially those that include return shipping coverage, can greatly boost customer trust and loyalty.

OEM VS AFTERMARKET

The inclusion of specific part numbers suggests a balanced blend of OEM and aftermarket parts. Moreover, there's a notable prevalence of generic listings labeled as "Does Not Apply," which presents an opportunity for optimization in search engine visibility by effectively supplying this information.

MANUFACTURER WARRANTY: A KEY DIFFERENTIATOR

A 1-year warranty is the most common among listings, followed by 2-year warranties. Highlighting your warranty terms, especially if they are competitive, can be a strong selling point.

THE RICHES ARE IN THE NICHES

Focusing on top-selling products, tweaking prices strategically, offering competitive return and warranty policies, meeting different product needs, and leveraging regional strengths can really boost sellers' performance in the competitive car struts market.

Headlight Hustle: The eBay Car Parts Niche That Could Light Up Your Business

eBay Motors is a popular destination for car parts and accessories, and headlights stand out as a preferred category among DIY mechanics across the country. Let's explore further by examining the headlights section on eBay Motors, focusing on popular items, pricing patterns, and potential market opportunities for sellers aiming to establish themselves in this field.

OVERVIEW OF THE EBAY MOTORS HEADLIGHTS CATEGORY

In eBay Motors, the headlights category offers a wide array of products tailored to different vehicle models and consumer tastes. Known for its high sales volume, this category shows a steady demand from both car owners and enthusiasts.

POPULAR PRODUCTS AND TRENDS

LED Headlights: Leading the market with their energy efficiency and long lifespan, LED headlights are a preferred option for many consumers.

Projector Headlights: Recognized for their precise illumination, projector headlights have gained popularity, particularly among owners of contemporary vehicles.

Halo Headlights: Providing both style and improved visibility, halo headlights maintain appeal to a dedicated but niche customer base.

PRICE RANGES AND CONSUMER PREFERENCES

In the headlights category, prices vary widely, catering to both budget-conscious shoppers and those looking for premium products. More affordable options usually fall between $30 and $100, while high-end models can go for over $200. Success in this category hinges on grasping the target customer segment and matching product offerings to their particular requirements and financial limits.

SUPPLY VS DEMAND

High price point niches generate more $ Sales in Headlights

There is a high concentration of listings in the lower price ranges, particularly in the first price segment, suggesting that most of the supply is at lower price points.

The number of listings seems to decrease as the price increases.

There are a few listings at higher price points with relatively high weekly sales, suggesting that while they are less common, they can generate significant revenue.

The dispersion of the blue dots suggests that there is variability in how much each listing sells per week, regardless of the price point.

It seems that listings in the mid-price ranges have a higher weekly sales volume compared to those at the lowest price point, indicating potential for higher revenue in those segments despite a lower supply.

There's a noticeable gap in listings at certain higher price points, which might indicate a market opportunity or a niche with less competition.

OPPORTUNITIES FOR NEW SELLERS

Specialized Headlight Assemblies: Customized or model-specific headlight assemblies present a lucrative opportunity, especially for sellers who can cater to particular vehicle makes and models.

Innovative Lighting Solutions: With technology constantly evolving, there is a growing market for headlights featuring advanced lighting technologies, such as adaptive lighting systems that adjust to driving conditions.

Sustainable Options: Eco-friendly headlights, such as those with low power consumption and longer life spans, are becoming increasingly popular, tapping into the environmentally conscious consumer segment.

Aftermarket Upgrades: Providing aftermarket solutions that enhance both the functionality and aesthetic appeal of headlights can attract car enthusiasts looking to personalize their vehicles.

STRATEGIES FOR SUCCESS

Invest in Higher Priced Products and meet the needs of a new buyer instead of price wars with the rest of the category sellers

Market Research: Keep abreast of the latest trends and consumer preferences within the headlights category.

Quality and Compliance: Ensure that products sourced meet safety standards and are compliant with vehicle regulations.

Customer Engagement: Utilize customer feedback to refine product offerings and improve customer service.

The headlights category in eBay Motors presents a dynamic and profitable market for new and existing sellers. By staying informed about market trends, understanding customer preferences, and leveraging the opportunities identified, sellers can successfully navigate this space and drive their business forward. Whether it's through innovative product offerings, catering to niche markets, or offering value-for-money solutions, the key to success lies in aligning with consumer needs and staying ahead of the curve.

Private label

A private label is when one company makes a product but sells it under another company's brand name. Retailers use private labels to offer unique items, expand their product range, and compete with other brands on pricing.

Even though private label products might look similar to ones already on the shelves, they have to have their own unique recipe or formula. For example, if a company sells chocolate chip cookies under its private label, the recipe won't be exactly the same as any other brand's. This rule applies to many different types of products, like electronics, jewelry, clothes, and pet food.

How does private labeling work?

Private labeling involves two main types of companies:

1. Private-label manufacturers: These companies work with businesses to develop and produce products.

2. Private-label sellers: These companies brand, market, and sell private-label products to retail customers.

A reliable private-label manufacturer focuses on ensuring product quality and managing production costs efficiently.

On the other hand, a savvy private-label seller focuses on building brand reputation, effective marketing, and establishing a profitable pricing strategy.

Private labels vs. white-label products

Private-label goods are distinct from white-label goods. While both involve a third-party manufacturer producing items for a retailer, there's a crucial difference.

In white-labeling, a manufacturer creates generic products in bulk and sells them to various retailers, who then sell them under their own brand names.

In contrast, private-label product lines are unique and exclusively available through a single retailer, like Costco's Kirkland Signature or Amazon's Basics range. White-label products, however, are generic and sold under the brands of multiple retailers.

The Benefits of Private Labeling

Private labeling offers advantages for both manufacturers and retailers, such as higher profit margins and greater control over branding.

Advantages of Private Labeling:

1. Unique Product Offering: Private labelers have the freedom to create and sell their own products, separate from established brands. This allows entrepreneurs to explore innovative

product ideas without being restricted by market trends.

2. Increased Profit Margins: Private-label products often generate higher profit margins compared to resale items. Retailers can set higher prices for their unique private-label products or leverage their brand influence to lower marketing expenses.

3. Control Over Pricing: Private labelers have the flexibility to adjust pricing strategies based on factors like market demand, production costs, and brand positioning.

4. Tailored Marketing Efforts: Private labelers can customize marketing campaigns to target specific audiences and align with their brand image. This flexibility enables them to adapt advertising strategies and promotional activities accordingly.

5. Adaptability: Private labeling allows for swift product development and adjustment to changing market trends and consumer preferences. This adaptability helps private labelers respond promptly to market demands and maintain competitiveness.

Private labeling empowers retailers, particularly smaller businesses, to offer premium products that might otherwise be challenging to develop independently. Moreover, depending on production scale and customization level, manufacturers can provide private-label products at competitive prices compared to resale alternatives.

Customized Pricing Control

Private-label sellers and manufacturers have the freedom to adjust manufacturing costs and pricing strategies for their product lines. This allows them to experiment with different pricing formulas to maximize profit margins.

Customized Marketing Control

As a private-label retailer, you have the flexibility to choose the marketing campaigns used to promote your branded products. Unlike national brands, you're not restricted by rigid or outdated marketing strategies.

Adaptability

Established brands often take months or even years to change their product formulas, pricing structures, or marketing approaches. In contrast, private-label sellers can adapt quickly in response to factors like negative feedback or low sales. This agility allows them to refine their products and pricing strategies to meet market demands efficiently.

Drawbacks of Private Labeling

Despite its benefits, private labeling also has its drawbacks, including the risk of inconsistent products and the challenge of building a brand from scratch.

Dependence on Third-Party Manufacturers

A significant drawback of private labeling is the reliance on third-party manufacturers. Any issues faced by the manufacturer, such as production delays or quality concerns, directly affect the private-label seller. This can lead to stock shortages, customer dissatisfaction, and potential damage to the brand's reputation.

Limited Innovation Scope

When working with private-labeling services, retailers may encounter limitations in product customization options. Depending on suppliers and product categories, retailers may not have as much control over the product design process as desired. However, establishing a close relationship with the manufacturer can help mitigate issues with product design and potentially facilitate customized research and development.

Examples of Private Label Products

Did you know that many everyday products and well-known brands are actually made by private-label companies? This business approach is used across various product types, whether they're sold online or in traditional stores.

Here are some examples of private-label products:

1. Coffee: Online, private-label coffee brands have become quite popular. These brands often work with coffee dropshippers who promptly ship orders once they're received.

2. Pet Food: Numerous online pet stores offer private-label pet food produced by large manufacturers serving multiple clients.

3. LED Lights: Online marketplaces offer a wide selection of private-label LED lights, sourced from a handful of manufacturers but with minor design differences.

4. Phone Accessories: Many third-party phone accessories like chargers and cases are made

by private-label companies and sold under various brand names.

5. Apparel: Online clothing retailers frequently collaborate with private-label garment manufacturers to create shirts, dresses, shoes, handbags, and more. These manufacturers often offer customization options such as printing custom designs on clothing and providing tailored services.

6. Smart Backpacks: Smart backpacks with features like device charging capabilities and built-in speakers are becoming increasingly popular online. Retailers can work with private-label manufacturers to develop customized smart backpacks for their customers.

7. Personal Care Products: A wide range of personal care items, from mouthwash to makeup, are sourced from manufacturers that serve private-label clients. Although the formulas may be customized, these products are usually produced on the same assembly lines.

Choosing the Right Private-Label Manufacturer

Before you pick a manufacturer, it's crucial to understand your target customers' buying habits. This will help you create compelling proposals for potential private-label brands. Attend networking events, trade shows, and other industry gatherings to learn more about your products, expand your network, and size up the competition. Also, think about patenting your idea to protect it from competitors who might create similar products.

While many people choose Amazon as their private-label manufacturer, it's worth exploring manufacturers that specialize in your specific products. For instance, instead of relying solely on a broad marketplace, Vega Coffee partnered with ice cream manufacturers and other coffee brands.

You can find potential partners at trade shows organized by the Private Label Manufacturers Association. Alternatively, you can search online for other options.

Popular Private-Label Manufacturers

1. Alibaba: This massive website makes it easy to find products from around the world. It connects brands with manufacturers that can

make a wide range of items, from electronics to cookware.

2. Wholesale2b: This online platform lists top dropshipping suppliers. With dropshipping, manufacturers take care of shipping, so you don't need to worry about storing products or shipping them yourself.

3. Worldwide Brands: Founded in 1999, Worldwide Brands researches third-party manufacturers and provides their details to subscribers. It's a helpful resource for finding the right private-label manufacturer for your needs.

4. Carlsberg Group: Carlsberg Group, known as one of the biggest brewery companies worldwide, provides private-label manufacturing services for retailers and businesses interested in crafting personalized beer and beverage items.

5. Teami Blends: Teami Blends is a company that makes wellness and skincare products. They're famous for their detox teas and natural skincare solutions. They offer options for businesses to have their own brand on these products, called white-label and private-label options.

6. Sunfood: This company makes organic superfoods and health products. They offer personalized options for retailers and brands, including custom formulation, packaging, and branding solutions.

Some of the best-selling products on eBay

Here, we are going to explore some of the top-selling items on eBay. Have it in mind that this will not remain constant as there could be new interest that may spring out.

Cables: The Unseen Heroes

In an age where technology is ubiquitous, it's no surprise that cables have become one of the best-selling products on eBay. With a sell-through rate (STR) of 38,680%, cables are not just a necessity but a hot commodity. The average listing makes at least 300 online sales in 30 days, showcasing the high demand for these essential items. From USB charging cables to those for musical instruments, the variety is vast, though it's worth noting the highly competitive nature of this market.

Fashion: A Timeless Demand

Men's clothing follows closely, boasting an impressive STR of 17,700% with an average price of $13.19. With over 13 million listings, the fashion category remains a staple in the top-selling charts. The success rate of these listings is high, with 89% making at least one sale. This indicates a consistent demand for apparel and the opportunity for sellers to tap into this evergreen market.

Tech Gadgets: The Smart Choice

Electronics never go out of style, and eBay's marketplace is proof of that. Smartphone accessories and tech gadgets continue to be a focal point for consumers. Items like phone cases, AirPod cases, and other related accessories are in high demand. Also, smartphones, laptops, gaming consoles, and smartwatches are among the best items to flip on the platform. These products attract gadget enthusiasts and offer sellers a lucrative opportunity, provided they source their inventory wisely and price competitively.

Home and Lifestyle: Comfort and Aesthetics

The home decor category has seen a surge in popularity, with items like wall art and holiday decor becoming increasingly sought after. This trend reflects a broader consumer interest in personalizing living spaces, making home decor a promising category for sellers on eBay.

Fitness Frenzy: Wellness on the Rise

Fitness products have also carved out a significant niche on eBay. Sports bras, athletic shorts, and yoga mats are just a few examples of items that have gained traction. The growing focus on health and wellness has propelled this category forward, offering sellers a chance to cater to a health-conscious audience.

Pet Love: Furry Friends First

Pet products, including bowls, collars, and beds, have become best sellers as well. The love for pets transcends the digital divide, and eBay sellers can find success by offering high-quality, innovative pet products that cater to the needs of pet owners.

Automotive Parts: The Need for Speed

Automotive parts, such as exterior parts, wheels, tires, and car lights, have also found their place among the best selling items on eBay. The automotive category attracts a niche but dedicated group of consumers looking to enhance or maintain their vehicles.

Collectibles: Nostalgia and Novelty

Collectibles, ranging from toys to sports memorabilia and even NFTs, continue to pique the interest of buyers. This category's success is driven by the emotional value and the potential for items to appreciate over time.

Jewelry and Watches: Timeless Elegance

Jewelry and watches continue to be symbols of elegance and status. Their enduring popularity on eBay underscores the platform's ability to provide valuable and luxurious items to a broad audience.

Massagers

From handheld options to powerful thumpers, these are hot sellers on eBay. Various brands are available, with some outperforming others, but overall, they boast high demand and quick turnover.

Lightsabers

Look for Hasbro lightsabers, particularly those from the early 2000s, though newer models from 2016 to 2023 also sell well. You can often find them in thrift stores for $1 to $3, and they typically sell for anywhere between $15 and $45, depending on their complexity. Basic models tend to fetch around $15."

Baseball Mitts and Gloves

Often overlooked, but with the season approaching, demand is set to soar, especially during the holiday season. Focus on pro models, with larger sizes (11 to 12.5 inches) having a quicker turnover. Smaller sizes may linger longer on shelves. Explore various brands for the best options, but be prepared to do some digging.

Remote Controls

With a vast customer base, sellers are raking in tens of thousands of dollars, and some even reach up to $100,000 solely from selling remote controls. Explore various brands for lucrative opportunities in this market."

Sports Cards

Despite past skepticism, the sports card market experienced a significant surge fueled by factors like Zion Williamson's entrance into the league, Gary Vaynerchuk's endorsements, and the pandemic-driven rise in at-home collecting. Prices skyrocketed, with cards valued at $6 now fetching $50, and those once priced at $50 now going for $480 or even $3500. While the market has cooled, there's still ample opportunity for savvy sellers. It may require a bit more patience and effort, but with diverse brands available, thorough research can lead to profitable sales.

Vacuum Cleaner Parts

Enjoying robust sales, vacuum cleaner parts present a lucrative niche, particularly for those not keen on selling full-sized vacuums. A complete vacuum purchased for $45 can yield higher profits when its parts are sold individually, such as the motor fetching $40 and the head selling for $50 or $60."

Receivers and Amplifiers

Often overlooked due to their weight, these items can be acquired for $15 to $40 but fetch solid prices ranging from $80 to $150 plus shipping. Note that USPS ground advantage shipping may require customers to pay an additional 40%.

People are willing to pay what they feel the item is worth, so I not only profit from the item itself but also from the shipping charges. This category and its items are often overlooked. The same holds true for DVD VCR combo players and VHS players. These items sell rapidly, are not always easy to find, and have a high failure rate, which dissuades many from investing in them.

Car Stereos

Testing these items might raise questions for some. However, if you can locate the wires, testing is straightforward. Alternatively, you can list them as parts to avoid the testing process altogether."

Digital Cameras

Despite the prevalence of smartphones, digital cameras remain a lucrative item to sell on eBay. They often sell within two to four weeks of listing and can fetch significant profits. With a variety of brands available, there's ample opportunity to make good money. Even broken cameras have a market, with prices ranging from $15 to $30, and many selling between $25 and $30 after being purchased for as little as $5. The demand and sell-through rate for digital cameras are remarkable."

Blender Cups

While bigger brands dominate, smaller ones also find buyers. Similar to blender cups, coffee makers are popular items, with some brands fetching over $100, including shipping.

Sunglasses and Eyeglass Frames

This category offers daily sales potential on platforms like eBay and Poshmark. Even frames with damaged lenses can be sold by listing them as 'frames only,' typically priced around $20 to $25. Despite needing replacement lenses, these items still attract buyers who are willing to customize them. Selling eyeglasses and sunglasses alone can yield substantial monthly earnings.

Air Purifiers and Humidifiers

In demand, especially during cold and flu season, these items typically fetch $50 to $60 plus shipping. Whether branded or unbranded, they sell consistently. Don't overlook the potential of selling air purifiers and humidifiers.

Bats

You gotta check out this category 'cause bats sell really well. Baseball, softball, T-ball bats—all of 'em can be found for under $5 and sold for $20 to $40, sometimes even $130! Usually, longer and heavier bats sell better, but not always. Like, some have a drop 10, others just drop three. Listing bats is easier than you think. Many have model numbers, so you just type that in, match the length and weight, then kinda tweak someone else's listing to fit yours.

Let's not forget about golf clubs. While you might want to skip over most of them, focus on the name brand ones, especially the newer models. Drivers are hot sellers. And don't overlook sand wedges and pitching wedges—they fly off the shelves faster than regular irons. Personally, I sell 99% of my golf clubs individually, even if I get a complete set. It's a bit slower, but it's consistent Income coming in every day, every week, helping to keep my store cushioned with fast-selling items.

Hair, Beauty Tools, and Equipment

Wanna grab loads of flat irons, blow dryers, and curling irons? Steer clear of Conair and Remington unless it's a Wet 2 Straight. But keep an eye out for BabyLiss Pro, HIS, GVP, and CHI—these are the ones that fly off the shelves.

3
How to create compelling and optimized listings that converts.

If you want to sell your items on eBay, you need to create attractive and effective listings that will catch the attention of potential buyers and convince them to buy from you. In this chapter, we will share some tips and best practices on how to write catchy titles, descriptions, and keywords, how to take and edit high-quality photos, how to choose the right category, condition, and price, and how to use eBay's tools and features to boost your visibility and sales.

Titles

The title is the first thing that buyers see when they browse or search for items on eBay. It should be clear, concise, and relevant to what you are selling. A good title should include the following elements:

- The brand name of the item, if applicable

- The model or style of the item, if applicable

- The size, color, or other important features of the item

- The condition of the item (new, used, refurbished, etc.)

- Any keywords that buyers might use to search for your item

For example, a good title for a pair of shoes might be:

- ❖ Nike Air Jordan 1 Retro High OG Men's Shoes Size 10 Black/Red New

This title includes the brand name, the model, the size, the color, and the condition of the shoes. It also uses keywords that buyers might use to find this item, such as "Nike", "Air Jordan", "Retro", "High", "OG", etc.

A bad title for the same pair of shoes might be:

- ❖ Shoes for sale

This title is too vague and does not describe what kind of shoes you are selling. It does not include any of the elements mentioned above. It will not attract buyers or rank well in search results.

Descriptions

The description is where you can provide more details about your item and persuade buyers to purchase it. A good description should include the following elements:

- A brief introduction that summarizes what you are selling and why buyers should buy from you.
- A detailed description that covers all the features and benefits of your item.
- A clear explanation of the condition of your item and any flaws or defects it might have.
- A list of what is included in your package (such as accessories, manuals, warranty cards, etc.)
- A statement of your return policy and shipping options. A call to action that invites buyers to place their bids or make their offers

For example, a good description for the same pair of shoes might be:

Welcome to my listing for a brand new pair of Nike Air Jordan 1 Retro High OG Men's Shoes in Size 10. These shoes are 100% authentic and come with the original box and receipt. They are one of the most iconic and sought-after sneakers in history. Don't miss this chance to own a piece of sneaker culture!

These shoes feature a classic black and red colorway that pays homage to the original Air Jordan 1 that Michael Jordan wore in 1985. They are made of premium leather and have a high-top silhouette that provides ankle support and comfort. They also have a rubber outsole that offers traction and durability.

These shoes are in brand new condition and have never been worn or tried on. They have no flaws or defects whatsoever. They come from a smoke-free and pet-free home.

The package includes:

- One pair of Nike Air Jordan 1 Retro High OG Men's Shoes in Size 10

- One original box with matching label

- One original receipt from Nike.com

- One pair of extra laces

I accept returns within 30 days of delivery as long as the shoes are in the same condition as they were received. The buyer is responsible for return shipping costs. I ship within one business day of receiving cleared payment via USPS Priority Mail with tracking and insurance. I only ship to confirmed addresses within the United States.

If you have any questions or concerns, please feel free to contact me. I will respond as soon as possible. Thank you for your interest in my listing. Please check out my other items for more great deals on sneakers and clothing. Happy bidding!

How to Take and Edit High-Quality Photos for eBay

If you want to sell your items on eBay, you need to take and edit high-quality photos that showcase their features and condition. Photos are the first thing that buyers look at, so they can make or break your listing. On eBay, you can include up to 24 photos in your listing. Additionally, you have the option to incorporate a video, though it's essential to adhere to eBay's policy regarding images, videos, and text.

Ensure that your photos and videos primarily showcase the product, with a preference for lifestyle imagery demonstrating the product in use. Aim to create videos that emulate user-generated content (UGC), characterized by its authenticity and lack of professional polish. Despite its amateur nature, UGC carries more credibility as it originates from everyday individuals rather than marketing agencies employing CGI.

Using user-generated content (UGC) boosts the trustworthiness of your listings. For example, if you're marketing drones, contemplate producing a video showcasing the drone in flight, offering prospective buyers a direct glimpse of its functionalities.

Here are some tips on how to take and edit high-quality photos for eBay.

1. Use a good camera. You don't need a professional DSLR, but you do need a camera that can capture clear and detailed images. A smartphone camera can work well, as long as it has a high resolution and a good lens. Avoid using a webcam or a low-quality digital camera, as they will produce blurry and grainy photos.

2. Choose a plain background. You want your item to stand out, not the background. A plain background will also make it easier to edit your photos later. You can use a white sheet, a poster board, or a wall as your background. Avoid using patterns, textures, or colors that will distract from your item.

3. Use natural light. Natural light is the best for taking photos, as it will show the true colors and details of your item. Try to take your photos near a window or outside, but avoid direct sunlight, as it will create harsh shadows and glare. If you have to use artificial light, use a softbox or a lamp with a white bulb, and avoid using the flash, as it will create reflections and wash out your item.

4. Take multiple photos from different angles. You want to show your item from every possible perspective, so that buyers can see its features and condition. Take photos from the front, back, sides, top, and bottom of your item. Also, take close-up photos of any important details, such as labels, tags, logos, defects such as stains, scratches or damage, or accessories. Avoid using filters, stickers, text or logos that may obscure or alter your item's appearance. You can upload up to 12 photos per listing on eBay, so make use of them.

5. Edit your photos. After you have taken your photos, you may need to edit them to make them look more professional and appealing. You can use a photo editing software or app on your computer or smartphone, such as

Photoshop, Lightroom, Snapseed, or VSCO. Some of the things you can do to edit your photos are:

- Crop your photos to remove any unnecessary space or distractions around your item.

- Rotate or straighten your photos to make sure they are aligned properly.

- Adjust the brightness, contrast, saturation, and sharpness of your photos to make them look more vivid and clear.

- Resize your photos to fit the eBay requirements. The minimum size is 500 pixels on the longest side, and the maximum size is 7 MB per photo.

- Save your photos in JPEG format with high quality settings.

How to Choose the Right Category, Condition, and Price Selling on eBay

If you are thinking of selling your items on eBay, you might be wondering how to choose the right category, condition, and price for your listings. These factors can make a big difference in how quickly and how much you sell. Here are some tips to help you make the best decisions for your eBay business.

Category: The category is the first thing that buyers see when they browse or search for items on eBay. It helps them narrow down their options and find what they are looking for. You should choose the most specific and relevant category for your item, based on its type, brand, model, features, etc. For example, if you are selling a pair of Nike Air Jordan sneakers, you should list them under Clothing, Shoes & Accessories > Men > Men's Shoes > Athletic Shoes. If you are not sure which category to choose, you can use the category finder tool on eBay or look at similar items that have sold recently. Choosing the right category for your item is important. eBay has thousands of categories and subcategories, so you need to do some research to find the most relevant one for your item. Some items can fit into more than one category, so you can use the advanced listing tool to list your item in up to two categories for an extra fee. This can increase your exposure and chances of selling.

Condition: The condition of your item is another factor that affects how buyers perceive your listing. eBay has four main condition categories: new, refurbished, used, and for parts or not working. You need to be honest and accurate about the condition of your item, as this can affect your seller reputation and feedback. You should also include clear photos and a detailed description of any flaws or defects. If your item is new or refurbished, you should provide proof of authenticity or warranty information. If your item is used or for parts, you should describe its functionality and any accessories or parts that are included or missing. Violating eBay's listing policies by misrepresenting a product's condition can result in account suspension. Furthermore, buyers have the right to dispute purchases if items don't match their descriptions. Honesty is the best policy; accurately describe used items to avoid complications.

Price: The price of your item is the final factor that determines how attractive your listing is to buyers. You need to set a fair and competitive price that reflects the market value of your item. You can use eBay's pricing guidance tool to get an estimate of what similar items have sold for recently. You can also check the completed listings and sold items filters to see the actual prices that buyers have paid for similar items. You can choose to list your item as an auction or a fixed price. Auctions can generate more interest and bidding wars, but they also have more uncertainty and risk. Fixed price listings can give you more control and convenience, but they also have more fees and competition. Fixed-price listings are ideal for selling brand-new items, while auctions are better suited for rare, discontinued items. Take, for instance, an antique comic book, which typically fares better in an auction format. Conversely, a newly manufactured t-shirt typically sells more effectively at a fixed price, unless it happens to be a limited edition product. Auctions thrive for rare items due to heightened demand exceeding supply, encouraging buyers to bid higher than usual. Take time to weigh the advantages and disadvantages of each option before making a decision. Opt for the one that aligns best with your objectives and personal preferences.

How to price your products for maximum profit and sales

Creating and optimizing listings on eBay can be overwhelming. It involves tasks like crafting appealing product images, writing compelling descriptions, and setting competitive prices to boost sales.

Among these tasks, finding the right pricing strategy can be daunting. Although your aim is to make a profit, setting prices too high may turn off buyers, while setting them too low could raise concerns about quality.

Since the price of an item greatly influences purchasing decisions, striking the right balance is crucial. Here's a guide to help you navigate the complexities of pricing your eBay listings.

Before diving into strategies, it's important to understand why pricing effectively on eBay is challenging. Pricing reflects the value you place on your products, balancing between premium pricing and budget-friendly options.

Accurate pricing is crucial because it heavily influences purchasing decisions. Studies show that pricing is one of the top factors affecting sales. Unlike other tactics like advertising, pricing has the most significant impact on profits. Even a small improvement in pricing can lead to a significant increase in profits.

Setting prices shouldn't be arbitrary; it requires a strategic approach that aligns with your product's value proposition. Start by conducting thorough research to understand the pricing landscape and determine a profitable range.

Understand Your Costs

Before setting a price, you need to fully understand your costs. This includes both direct costs like materials and labor, and indirect costs such as overhead, marketing, and shipping. Knowing your costs is the foundation of pricing because it ensures that you're not selling your products at a loss.

Know Your Market

Research your target market to understand what customers are willing to pay, as well as what your competitors are charging. Pricing too high can make you non-competitive, while pricing too low can devalue your product in the eyes of consumers. Some people have got a lot of time at their disposal that they can sit and browse all day long, searching and comparing. If you did not conduct proper market research, you may find yourself not doing well.

Target market requires a deep dive into demographics, psychographics, and consumer behavior.

Knowing your target market is not just about understanding who they are, but also why they choose to buy from you. eBay, being a vast marketplace, caters to a wide variety of customers, but not all of them will be interested in your products. By focusing on a specific segment, you can tailor your approach to meet their specific needs, desires, and expectations, thereby increasing the likelihood of sales.

Creating a Buyer Persona

A buyer persona is a semi-fictional representation of your ideal customer based on market research and real data about your existing customers. When creating a buyer persona, consider factors such as:

- Demographics: Age, gender, income level, education, occupation.

- Psychographics: Interests, hobbies, values, attitudes, lifestyle.

- Behavior: Buying patterns, brand loyalty, product usage.

This persona will guide you in customizing your marketing strategy to address the specific needs, behaviors, and concerns of your target market.

Consider the Perceived Value

The perceived value of your product plays a crucial role in pricing. If your product offers unique benefits or superior quality compared to competitors, you can price higher. Understand the value proposition of your product from the customer's perspective.

Employ Pricing Strategies

There are various pricing strategies you can employ, such as:

- Penetration Pricing: Setting a lower price to enter a competitive market and attract customers.

- Premium Pricing: Setting a high price to reflect the exclusivity or high quality of a product.

- Psychological Pricing: Using prices that have a psychological impact, like $19.99 instead of $20.

- Bundle Pricing: Offering a set of products at a lower price than if they were purchased individually.

Test and Adjust

Pricing isn't set in stone. Test different prices and monitor how they affect sales and profits.

Be prepared to adjust your prices based on market conditions, cost changes, and consumer feedback.

Communicate Value

Ensure that your pricing strategy is communicated effectively. Highlight the quality, benefits, and value of your product to justify the price point.

Monitor Regularly

The market is always changing, and so should your prices. Regularly review your pricing strategy to ensure it remains optimal.

By following these steps, you can set a price that not only covers your costs and earns a profit but also matches the perceived value of your product, ensuring maximum sales. Remember, the right price is a balance between your business needs and what the market can bear.

Pricing Strategies for eBay Sellers: Maximizing Profit and Sales

In the competitive marketplace of eBay, pricing your products effectively is crucial for maximizing profits and sales. The right pricing strategy can make the difference between a thriving business and one that struggles to gain traction. Here's a comprehensive guide to help eBay sellers navigate the complexities of pricing.

Understanding Your Market

Before setting prices, it's essential to understand the market dynamics for your products. Research similar items on eBay to gauge the average selling price. Utilize eBay's pricing recommendations tool as a starting point. This tool provides an average price range based on similar listings, helping you to position your products competitively.

Auction or Fixed-Price Listings?

eBay offers two primary listing options: auctions and fixed-price listings. Your choice should depend on the type of product you're selling and your sales objectives.

Auctions are ideal for unique or high-demand items where the market can drive the price higher than a set amount. In an auction-style listing, potential buyers bid on your product over a set period, typically ranging from one to ten days. However, ensure you set a reserve price to avoid selling below your minimum acceptable price.

Fixed-Price listings are suitable for items you wish to sell in volume. This method allows you to set a consistent profit margin and offers ease for buyers to make a purchase immediately without the uncertainty of bidding.

You can list multiple quantities for durations of 10 days, 30 days, or until manually canceled. Additionally, the 'Best Offer' feature is available, enabling buyers to submit offers based on their willingness to pay, which you can then accept or counter.

Pricing Psychology and Strategy

Pricing isn't just about covering costs and adding a profit margin; it's also about psychology. Consider the following strategies:

- Charm Pricing: Setting prices just below a round number (e.g., $19.99 instead of $20) can make a price seem significantly lower.

- Anchor Pricing: Displaying a higher original price next to the selling price can create a sense of value and urgency.

- Bundle Pricing: Offering multiple items together at a discounted rate can increase the perceived value and encourage bulk purchases.

Repricing Strategy

The market is dynamic, and so should be your pricing. Regularly adjust your prices in response to market changes, competitor pricing, and inventory levels. Consider using a repricing tool to automate this process and stay competitive.

Incorporating Expenses

Your pricing should account for all expenses, including eBay fees, shipping costs, and taxes. This ensures that your profit margins are accurate and sustainable.

Negotiated Prices

Be open to accepting offers from buyers. This can increase the likelihood of a sale and clear inventory faster, especially for items that have been listed for a while.

key points to remember when setting your eBay prices:

1. Avoid setting prices based solely on your personal goals or desires.

2. Refrain from guessing what shoppers might be willing to pay for your product.

3. Don't wait until after sourcing to determine if a product is profitable.

Add the shipping details

Similar to other online selling platforms, you have the option to include shipping details for your products, but this is applicable only for fixed-price listings. For auctions, shipping arrangements are typically discussed between you and the buyer after the auction concludes.

You can opt for either domestic or international shipping and decide whether to offer flat-rate or free shipping. Additionally, you can customize shipping rates using shipping tables based on various locations and weights.

If you prefer not to ship to certain countries, you can specify exclusions within the system.

As for the debate between free and paid shipping, there's no definitive answer. If shipping costs are minimal, you can incorporate them into your listing price or absorb them from your profit. Free shipping tends to attract more buyers for small items, while larger and heavier items typically necessitate charging shipping fees.

Before finalizing your listing, adjust your selling preferences, including:

- Buyer requirements such as location or order history

- Accepted payment methods

- Return and refund policies

- Item location

These preferences help filter out undesired buyers, especially those with a higher likelihood of fraudulent activity.

4
How to manage your inventory and shipping

If you run an online business, you know how important it is to manage your inventory and shipping processes. You want to make sure that your products are stored properly, shipped quickly, and delivered safely to your customers. You also want to keep track of your orders, update your inventory levels, and handle any issues that may arise, such as returns and refunds. In this chapter, we will explain how to organize and store your products, how to pack and ship them safely and efficiently, how to track and update your orders, and how to handle returns and refunds.

Organizing and storing your products

The first step in managing your inventory and shipping is to organize and store your products in a way that makes sense for your business. Depending on the type and size of your products, you may need different storage solutions, such as shelves, bins, racks, or boxes. You should also label your products clearly with their name, SKU, price, and quantity. This will help you find them easily when you need to pack and ship them.

You should also keep track of your inventory levels and update them regularly. You can use a spreadsheet, an app, or a software program to record your inventory data. You should also perform regular inventory audits to make sure that your records match your actual stock. This will help you avoid running out of stock or having excess inventory that takes up space and costs money.

Packing and shipping your products

The next step in managing your inventory and shipping is to pack and ship your products in a way that ensures their safety and quality. You should use appropriate packaging materials, such as boxes, envelopes, bubble wrap, tape, labels, etc. You should also choose the right size and weight of the package to avoid paying extra fees or damaging the product. You should also include a packing slip or an invoice with the order details, such as the customer's name, address, phone number, email, order number, product name, quantity, price, etc.

You should also choose the best shipping method for your business. You can use different carriers, such as USPS, FedEx, UPS, DHL, etc., depending on the cost, speed, reliability, and tracking options they offer. You should also compare the shipping rates and delivery times of different carriers and choose the one that suits your budget and customer expectations. You should also provide your customers with a tracking number or a confirmation email once you ship their order.

Tracking and updating your orders

The third step in managing your inventory and shipping is to track and update your orders as they progress through the shipping process. You should monitor the status of your orders using the tracking number or the confirmation email provided by the carrier. You should also update your inventory levels accordingly when you ship an order or receive a return. This will help you avoid overselling or underselling your products.

You should also communicate with your customers throughout the shipping process. You should send them a confirmation email when they place an order, a notification email when you ship their order, a delivery email when their order arrives, and a follow-up email to ask for feedback or reviews. You should also respond to any questions or concerns they may have about their order in a timely and professional manner.

Handling returns and refunds

The final step in managing your inventory and shipping is to handle any returns and refunds that may occur. You should have a clear and fair return policy that outlines the conditions and procedures for returning or exchanging a product. You should also display this policy on your website or in your confirmation email. You should also provide your customers with a return label or a return address if they need to send back a product.

You should also process any returns and refunds as quickly as possible. You should inspect the returned product for any damage or defect and issue a refund or an exchange accordingly. You should also update your inventory levels when you receive a return or send out an exchange. You should also notify your customer when you process their return or refund and thank them for their business.

Managing your inventory and shipping is an essential part of running an online business. It can help you improve your customer satisfaction, reduce your costs, increase your sales, and grow your business. By following these steps, you can organize and store your products, pack and ship them safely and efficiently, track and update your orders, and handle returns and refunds effectively.

5

How to provide excellent customer service and build your reputation

Customer service is one of the most important aspects of running a successful online business. It can make or break your reputation, and affect your sales, ratings, and reviews. In this chapter, we will share some advice on how to communicate with your buyers, how to respond to questions, feedback, and complaints, how to resolve disputes and cases, and how to earn positive ratings and reviews.

Communication is key

The first step to providing excellent customer service is to communicate clearly and professionally with your buyers. You should always use polite and respectful language, avoid slang or jargon, and check your spelling and grammar before sending a message. You should also respond promptly to any inquiries or messages from your buyers, preferably within 24 hours. This shows that you care about their needs and that you are reliable and trustworthy.

Some tips for effective communication are:

- Use a friendly and personal tone, but not too casual or informal. For example, you can start your message with "Hi [buyer's name]," and end it with "Thank you for choosing my shop," or "Have a great day."

- Provide as much information as possible, but not too much. For example, you can include the details of the order, the shipping method and tracking number, the estimated delivery date, and any special instructions or policies. However, you should avoid sending long paragraphs or unnecessary information that might confuse or overwhelm the buyer.

- Use bullet points or numbered lists to organize your information and make it easier to read.

- Use emojis or emoticons sparingly and appropriately. They can add some personality and warmth to your message, but they can also be misinterpreted or seen as unprofessional. You should only use them if they match your brand's voice and tone, and if they suit the context and purpose of your message.

- Confirm the buyer's satisfaction and ask for feedback. You can send a follow-up message after the order has been delivered, thanking the buyer for their purchase and asking them to leave a review or rating. You can also invite them to contact you if they have any questions or issues with their order.

Responding to questions, feedback, and complaints

Sometimes, you might receive questions, feedback, or complaints from your buyers. These can be positive or negative, depending on their experience with your product or service. You should always respond to these messages in a timely and respectful manner, regardless of their tone or content.

Some tips for responding to questions, feedback, and complaints are:

- Acknowledge the buyer's message and express your appreciation for their interest or feedback. For example, you can say "Thank you for your message," or "I appreciate your feedback."

- Answer any questions clearly and accurately. If you don't know the answer or need more time to find it out, let the buyer know that you are working on it and when you will get back to them.

- Address any feedback or complaints constructively and positively. If the buyer is happy with their order, thank them for their kind words and encourage them to shop with you again. If the buyer is unhappy with their order, apologize for their dissatisfaction and offer a solution or a compensation. For example, you can offer a refund, a replacement, an exchange, a discount, or a free gift.

- Avoid arguing or blaming the buyer for their feedback or complaint. Even if you think they are wrong or unreasonable, you should not get defensive or aggressive. Instead, try to understand their perspective and empathize with their feelings. You can say "I'm sorry to hear that you are not satisfied with your order," or "I understand your frustration."

- Keep calm and professional. Sometimes, you might encounter rude or abusive buyers who might insult you or your products. In these cases, you should not stoop to their level or retaliate. Instead, you should remain calm and professional, and report them to the platform if necessary.

Resolving disputes and cases

Occasionally, you might face disputes or cases from your buyers. These are formal complaints that are escalated to the platform's resolution center. They usually involve issues such as non-delivery, non-receipt, item not as described, item damaged in transit, unauthorized payment, etc.

Some tips for resolving disputes and cases are:

- Respond as soon as possible. You should not ignore or delay responding to a dispute or a case. This might worsen the situation and damage your reputation. You should try to resolve the issue directly with the buyer before it escalates further.

- Provide evidence and documentation. You should provide any relevant evidence and documentation that supports your position in the dispute or case. For example, you can provide proof of shipping, delivery confirmation, tracking information, photos of the item before shipping, screenshots of conversations with the buyer, etc.

- Cooperate with the platform's policies and procedures. You should follow the platform's policies and procedures for handling disputes and cases. You should also respect the platform's decision and outcome, even if you disagree with it.

- Learn from the experience and improve your practices. You should not take disputes and cases personally or let them discourage you. Instead, you should learn from the experience and improve your practices to prevent or minimize future issues. You can review your product descriptions, photos, prices, policies, shipping methods, packaging, etc., and make any necessary changes or improvements.

Earning positive ratings and reviews

Ratings and reviews are one of the most influential factors that affect your reputation and sales. They reflect your buyers' satisfaction and trust in your products and services. They also help other potential buyers to decide whether to buy from you or not.

Some tips for earning positive ratings and reviews are:

- Deliver high-quality products and services. You should always deliver what you promise and meet or exceed your buyers' expectations. You should ensure that your products are well-made, well-packaged, and well-presented.

You should also provide excellent customer service throughout the transaction.

- Ask for ratings and reviews politely and sincerely. You should not beg or bribe your buyers to leave ratings and reviews. Instead, you should ask them politely and sincerely, and explain how much you value their feedback. You can also offer incentives or rewards for leaving ratings and reviews, such as discounts, coupons, freebies, etc., as long as they are allowed by the platform's policies.

- Respond to ratings and reviews graciously and gratefully. You should always respond to ratings and reviews, whether they are positive or negative. You should thank your buyers for their feedback and show your appreciation. You should also address any issues or concerns that they might have raised in their feedback.

- Encourage repeat purchases and referrals. You should try to build long-term relationships with your buyers and turn them into loyal customers. You can do this by offering loyalty programs, referral programs, newsletters, social media updates, etc., that keep them engaged and informed about your products and services. You can also ask them to recommend you to their friends and family.

Customer service is not only a duty but also an opportunity to showcase your brand's personality, values, and professionalism. By providing excellent customer service, you can build your reputation, increase your sales, and grow your business. Remember that happy customers are the best advertisement for your business!

6

How to grow your EBay business and scale up your income

If you have been selling on eBay for a while, you might be wondering how to take your business to the next level. How can you increase your sales volume, attract more customers, and earn more profits? In this chapter, we will discuss some of the strategies and techniques that successful eBay sellers use to grow their business and scale up their income.

Cross-Sell and Upsell Your Products

One of the most effective ways to boost your sales is to cross-sell and upsell your products. Cross-selling means offering related or complementary items to your customers, such as accessories, add-ons, or upgrades. For example, if you sell laptops, you can cross-sell laptop cases, keyboards, mice, or headphones. Upselling means encouraging your customers to buy a higher-end or more expensive version of your product, such as a newer model, a larger size, or a premium edition. For example, if you sell cameras, you can upsell a camera with more features, better resolution, or extra lenses.

Cross-selling and upselling can help you increase your average order value, improve customer satisfaction, and build loyalty. To implement these techniques effectively, you need to understand your customers' needs and preferences, and offer them relevant and valuable options. You can also use tools like eBay's Promotions Manager to create and manage cross-sell and upsell offers on your listings.

Product Bundling

Another way to increase your sales volume is to bundle your products together. Bundling means selling two or more products as a package deal, usually at a lower price than buying them separately. For example, if you sell books, you can bundle books from the same author, genre, or series. Bundling can help you clear out your inventory faster, attract more buyers who are looking for a bargain, and create a sense of urgency and scarcity.

Discounts and promotions

You can also use discounts and promotions to boost your sales. Discounts and promotions are special offers that reduce the price of your products for a limited time or under certain conditions. For example, you can offer free shipping, coupons, buy-one-get-one-free deals, or seasonal sales. Discounts and promotions can help you increase your conversion rate, generate more traffic, and create repeat customers. However, you need to be careful not to overuse them or undercut your profit margin. You should also track and measure the results of your discounts and promotions to see what works best for your business.

Product range expansion

Besides increasing your sales volume, another way to grow your eBay business is to expand your product range. Expanding your product range means adding new products or categories to your existing offerings. For example, if you sell clothing, you can expand your product range by adding shoes, bags, jewelry, or other accessories. Expanding your product range can help you reach new markets, attract more customers, and increase your sales potential.

However, expanding your product range also comes with some challenges. You need to do market research to identify the demand and competition for the new products or categories. You also need to source the products from reliable suppliers, manage your inventory and storage space, and update your listings and marketing materials accordingly.

Diversify your income streams

Another way to grow your eBay business is to diversify your income streams. Diversifying your income streams means creating multiple sources of revenue from different channels or platforms. For example, if you sell physical products on eBay, you can diversify your income streams by selling digital products on other platforms like Etsy or Shopify. Digital products are items that can be downloaded or accessed online, such as eBooks, courses, software, or music.

Diversifying your income streams can help you reduce the risk of relying on one source of income that might fluctuate or decline over time. It can also help you leverage your existing skills and knowledge, reach new audiences, and increase your earning potential.

However, diversifying your income streams also requires more time and effort to manage multiple channels or platforms. You need to learn the rules and best practices of each platform, create and maintain different accounts and profiles, and monitor and optimize your performance across different channels.

Leveraging other platforms and tools

Finally, another way to grow your eBay business is to leverage other platforms and tools to market your business. Leveraging other platforms and tools means using external resources or services to promote your products or brand. For example, you can leverage social media platforms like Facebook, Instagram, or Pinterest to showcase your products, engage with your customers, and drive traffic to your EBay store. You can also leverage email marketing tools like Mailchimp or Aweber to build an email list of subscribers who are interested in your products or niche. You can then send them newsletters, updates, tips, or offers that will encourage them to buy from you.

Leveraging other platforms and tools can help you increase your visibility online, build trust and credibility with your audience, and generate more leads and sales for your eBay business.

However, leveraging other platforms and tools also requires more time and money to create and manage your content, campaigns, and analytics.

You need to choose the right platforms and tools that suit your business goals, target market, and budget.

You also need to test and tweak your strategies and tactics to see what works best for your business.

Growing your eBay business and scaling up your income is not an easy task, but it is possible if you apply some of the strategies and techniques we discussed in this chapter.

You can increase your sales volume by cross-selling, upselling,

bundling, and offering discounts and promotions.

You can expand your product range by adding new products or categories.

You can diversify your income streams by creating multiple sources of revenue from different channels or platforms.

And you can leverage other platforms and tools to market your business effectively.

By doing these things, you can take your EBay business to the next level and achieve your desired income goals.

Social media and e-commerce

Studies indicate that 98% of digital consumers engage with social media, with 74% trusting these platforms for purchasing decisions and 55% actively researching products on them. For eBay sellers, leveraging social media marketing can effectively capture early-stage customers and influence their buying decisions in favor of your products.

Despite the vast opportunities presented by various social networks and their ever-evolving features, the complexity can intimidate small businesses. To assist you in establishing your brand presence and expanding your customer base, we'll guide you through strategies to leverage social media to achieve your business objectives.

eBay's customer base consists predominantly of digital consumers. With a substantial following of nearly 13 million across our social channels, we have unparalleled access to online shoppers interested in our brand, all at a minimal cost.

Through platforms like eBay for Business on Facebook and YouTube, we engage with, inform, and support our sellers while also showcasing their success stories. Additionally, our consumer-oriented accounts on Facebook, Instagram, and Twitter play a vital role in directing traffic to our marketplace, highlighting the value and diversity of our inventory, sharing inspiring stories from sellers, and cultivating a sense of community by spotlighting unique eBay finds. To achieve our desired outcomes, we employ a combination of organic and paid social media strategies.

Organic and paid social

Organic Social Posts
When we talked Organic, we are referring to social media posts that are unpaid and haven't been boosted through payment. These posts when posted naturally surface in followers' feeds or timelines, reaching a broad, untargeted audience. Some brands employ organic posts to share general promotional or marketing messages. Although organic posts are effective for generating awareness and engagement without expenses, it is quite difficult to stand out amidst the multitude of

social media content and this could be demanding.

Paid Social Posts
These are boosted social media posts done by the user with monetary investment to ensure they reach a broader audience. These sponsored posts resemble traditional ads. Most brands or smaller business utilizes paid social posts to target particular consumers interested in specific products or categories, regardless of their follow status. The beauty of social platforms is that they are built with enhanced targeting options, one can precisely tailor messages to specific customer segments. Paid promotion is ideal for driving acquisition, fostering growth, and encouraging purchase decisions."

Social media marketing tips

There are many brands leveraging social media's potential. Businesses, irrespective of their scale or industry, utilize social platforms to reach new audiences and engage with existing customers. The beauty of social media marketing lies in its accessibility – it doesn't demand a hefty budget or extensive resources to kickstart. It's free and available to everyone. Whether you're a person who knows almost everything in social media marketing or someone who is just embarking on the journey, we've compiled essential tips that all businesses should consider.

- Establish your objectives from the start.

Whatever you intend to gain, whether to enhance brand visibility, promote products to a wider audience, drive traffic to your store or listings, or foster customer loyalty, you need to first establish your objectives.

Select your platforms wisely. Each platform offers unique strengths and caters to specific audiences, so align your choices with your goals. For tailored advice on each platform, visit our Seller Center Social Media page.

Create your accounts and choose your handles thoughtfully. Consistency is key, so ideally, your social media handle should match your eBay seller name. If unavailable, consider adding a prefix (like "The") or underscores for coherence.

Master posting best practices and utilize available tools. Countless resources are just a Google or YouTube search away. For example, eBay's social media managers stay abreast of trends via the comprehensive SocialBakers blog.

Grow your followers organically. Follow friends, competitors, and their followers. Avoid purchasing followers; it's not a worthwhile investment. Aim to cultivate a genuine and engaged follower base.

Craft engaging content. Observe what resonates with your audience and replicate successful strategies. Utilize analytic tools provided by platforms to understand engagement patterns. Focus on creating captivating visuals and leverage hashtags to boost visibility.

Direct traffic back to your eBay store and listings by incorporating links in your posts. Drive viewers directly to specific listings and include a link to your eBay store in your bio. Given the length of eBay links, consider using a link-shortening service like Bitly.

Expand your reach with ads. Begin with organic posts to grasp platform dynamics and identify effective content types. Once you're comfortable and experiencing some traction, experiment with paid marketing. Each platform offers tools for creating ads or boosting posts at minimal costs for initial insights. You can start with as little as a $10 investment to amplify your organic posts.

Enjoy the process! Allocate dedicated time for social media marketing and view it as an investment in your business. Utilize free publishing tools like Hootsuite to plan and schedule content in advance, making the process smoother and more efficient.

Marketing with videos

Video marketing is becoming more and more popular by the day making it a popular tool for adverts. Harness the power of video to engage buyers, convey your brand identity, and establish a stronger connection. Depending on your objectives, various types of videos can be effective:

- Check-ins: Provide followers with insights into your business through a "talking-head" style video, updating them on current developments.
- How-to videos: Ideal for demonstrating the purpose, value, or function of your inventory, showcasing your expertise as a seller.
- Behind-the-scenes videos: Offer customers a glimpse into your business operations or introduce them to your team, fostering a sense of familiarity and personal connection.
- Product-launch videos: Unveil new or upcoming products to generate anticipation and excitement among

customers, building awareness for your brand.

Highlight the distinctive products in your eBay store with unique-inventory videos! Share the special attributes or captivating backstories behind specific items to intrigue customers.

Video best practices vary depending on the platform where you choose to share them.

YouTube

YouTube, one of the best video sharing platform is a great platform for extended content, usually lasting from 3 to 5 minutes. Product demonstrations and instructional guides perform well on YouTube. Make sure your titles and descriptions include relevant keywords to improve search visibility, and consistently link back to your eBay store for easy navigation.

Facebook and Instagram

These two platforms are not like YouTube and therefore, you should aim to limit your Story segments to 15 seconds each. Alternatively, you can allow Instagram to automatically segment your story into 15-second clips.

Regardless of the video type, adopt the role of your own artistic director. Pay careful attention to each shot, ensuring a clutter-free background and attire that harmonizes with the surroundings. Position the camera angle favorably to present yourself in the most flattering light.

While the initial process may seem daunting, there's no need to rush for perfection in your first month on social media. Take your time and dedicate weekly intervals to pursuing your initial goals. As you gain insights into what resonates with your audience, gradually expand and refine your strategy.

Snapchat

Snapchat offers a platform for exploration, narrative, and interaction through its vibrant visual content. Snapchat allow users to seamlessly convert their eBay listings into engaging snaps right from the eBay app.

With a user base of over 347 million daily active users, Snapchat presents an opportunity to reach a new audience and explore untapped potential for your business.

With just a single tap, you can generate a Snapchat-ready design featuring listing details, an image, and a clickable link back to your eBay listing. Developed in collaboration with Snapchat, this new template produces a ready-to-share snap. Alternatively, you can use your creativity by adding stickers, text, and effects to make your listing stand out. Potential buyers can also utilize this feature to share snaps of items they're enthusiastic about with their Snapchat connections.

To explore this feature directly from your Active Listings or any listing on the eBay app:

- Ensure you're using the latest version of the eBay app and logged into Snapchat.
- Open the eBay app and select any listing.
- Tap the Share icon located at the top of a listing page or on the Active Listings page.
- Choose the Snapchat icon to instantly transition to the Snapchat Camera featuring the automated eBay sticker.
- From there, craft an original Snap using the eBay sticker, and enhance it with any of Snapchat's creative tools.

Conclusion

You have reached the end of this book, but not the end of your journey. In this book, you have learned how to start, grow, and scale your own eBay business. You have discovered the best practices, tips, and tools to succeed in the online marketplace. You have also learned how to avoid common pitfalls and overcome challenges that may arise along the way.

Selling on eBay is not only a profitable opportunity, but also a rewarding and fulfilling one. You can create your own brand, serve your customers, and make a positive impact on the world. You can also enjoy the flexibility, freedom, and fun of being your own boss.

But none of this will happen unless you take action. Don't let fear, doubt, or procrastination stop you from pursuing your dreams. The time to start is now. You have everything you need to succeed: a proven system, a supportive community, and a powerful platform.

So what are you waiting for? Go ahead and launch your first listing today. You have nothing to lose and everything to gain. Remember, the sky is the limit when it comes to selling on eBay. Thank you for reading this book and I wish you all the best in your eBay journey.

www.ingramcontent.com/pod-product-compliance
Lightning Source LLC
Chambersburg PA
CBHW031428210526
45464CB00005B/2104